RUSSIAN ARTIFICIAL INTELLIGE

March 2019

National Intelligence Estimate Scope of Analysis

Artificial Intelligence is both a disruptive and an assistive technology that will impact humanity in a profound manner.

As a matter of National Security, nations must ensure the cognitive capabilities of their nation's computing infrastructure evolves. Evolution must occur in their militaries, governing systems, election systems, critical infrastructures and those systems important to a freely communicating population.

Along with supporting our nation's technological cognitive evolution, we must also assess the status of an adversary nation's cognitive computing capability to understand the risk to our national security.

In this brief, Russia's Artificial Intelligence capabilities are assessed in the context of Kinetic Warfare, Cyber Warfare and Cyber supported Information Warfare

Words of Estimative Probability *(CIA,2008)*

Estimates of the probability of occurrence are derived from research of Open Source Intelligence (OSINT) material and a confidence level is applied to a statement of risk.

The confidence levels range from *Almost Certainly Not*, whereby there is zero expectation of success, to *Possible* which is the highest degree of expectation of success for the stated risk.

Almost Certainly Not	Probably Not	Even Chance	Probable	Almost Certain	Possible

Focus Issues and Summary Estimative Probability

A. *Russia will continue to improve its Artificial Intelligence knowledge:* Russia is increasing their scientific and academic communities' focus on AI development. Their strategy is to establish and strengthen relationships with U.S. AI research universities, academics and commercial entities who are advancing the science and practical use of AI. Using this collaborative approach, it is **almost certain** Russia will continue to advance its Artificial Intelligence knowledge.

B. *Russia will increase the use of Artificial Intelligence in their kinetic weapons:* Russia is actively working to incorporate AI into their kinetic weapons and are making progress. Even though most of their current and near-term AI architectures are focused on image recognition systems, it is **almost certain** they will continue to increase their use of AI in their kinetic weapons and expand their capabilities.

C. *Russia will incorporate AI to assist in command and control of weapons systems:* Along with fielding robotic systems like Unmanned Combat Vehicles, Russia is also fielding military command and control systems that contain some form of artificial intelligence, but it appears they are only focusing on the kinetic battlefield. It is **probable** they will expand their AI based C2 systems to include both the Cyber and kinetic battlefields.

Focus Issues and Summary Estimative Probability *(cont.)*

D. *Russia will independently develop AI assisted Cyber and Information Warfare systems:* At the core of the upcoming next generation of Cyber and Information Warfare will be Quantum Computing based Artificial Intelligence (QC-AI). When viewing their current capabilities in computer system research and their lack of advanced Cyber security development, it is believed they will ***probably not*** be able to independently develop the next generation of Artificial Intelligence based Cyber Weapons.

National Intelligence Estimate Purpose

Increasingly society is becoming highly dependent on computers to function freely and efficiently. Growing at a fast rate is the benefits computers bring to the new total warfare battlefield. Militaries are expanding their dependence on computers across the warfare spectrum. Computers are necessary from intelligence support systems to that of identifying, tracking and engaging enemies. As the military continues to discover the benefit of using computers to assist in warfare, the requirements for the computing systems continue to increase in scope. The dependency on computers is a natural evolution that has been occurring in the civilian sector for the last few decades. But the U.S. federal and military agencies late arrival to the computing sector and its low valuation of technology personnel means they must rely on the civilian sector to help defend against adversarial nations, such as Russia.

Russia understands that the battlefield is evolving from one where humans directly engage each other across clearly defined physical borders to one where borders between nations are only virtual. Due to the increasing virtualization of sovereign borders, weapons of war and defense are increasingly controlled by computers. Besides the growing use of computer assisted weapons physical weapons, like bullets and bombs, newer weapons designed to engage in Cyber and Information Warfare have been used effectively in attacks against the Ukraine, Estonia, England and United States. The new battlefield still includes traditional military forces, but now the militaries and intelligence agencies of nations can directly reach past other nation's borders directly into the daily lives of citizens in their homes. In fact, confrontation of other countries' citizens can occur just 16 inches in front of face on their computer. Also, due to the growing number of Internet connected devices in homes, innocent people can suffer Cyber-attack in various other ways.

Beyond human capacity, computers can process more information, at a faster rate, respond quicker and not fatigue. Also, computers can assist humans with their mundane, repetitive, exhausting and dangerous tasks. When it is required to analyze quantities of information beyond what is humanly possible, the computer's ability to accept, process, correlate and deliver a report can be a great value because it could provide an advantage over an adversary who doesn't have the same capabilities.

In typical computer programming, an output is based on inputs from a predefined range of possibilities. This is automation and computers have been programmed to do this very well. However, in areas such as intelligence and warfare, it is nearly impossible to know in advance all possible human actions and behaviors, let alone program in advance all the appropriate responses for all possible behaviors. Therefore, computers must be capable of learning behavior and then being able to apply the correct response for a given behavior. This "ability to acquire and apply knowledge and skills" is what the Oxford dictionary defines as intelligence.

To enable intelligence in computers, also known as Artificial Intelligence (AI), mathematical algorithms are used to classify inputs to help derive correct output. Since the science of artificial intelligence is a much broader discipline a primer on the technology is contained in Appendix A.

Russia clearly understands that a nation that ignores, resists or doesn't properly prioritize the assistive capabilities of Artificial Intelligence (AI) will find themselves at a strategic and tactical disadvantage militarily and in their intelligence capabilities. It is their political and military leadership's understanding of these facts that is motivating their nation's leadership to encourage and support the pursuit of AI research and development. Their primary objectives of AI are to gather and process intelligence information, control machines and implement widespread facial recognition systems.

It is important that our nation's federal and military agencies understand the threat Russia poses, especially with their intentions to adopt artificial intelligence. In addition, since U.S. research and development in AI is principally done by American companies, academic institutions, and independent researchers' they must appreciate that collaboration with Russia increases the potential to lose control of their intellectual capital and it enhances Russia's military strength, all of which has a negative impact on our national security.

Even though state and local and governments, along with their police agencies, do not collaborate, deliver services or engage in kinetic warfare with Russia, they have been targeted by attacks from their threat actors, so they need to understand the evolving threat from Russia in Cyberspace to help defend their environments against attacks.

The purpose of this NIE is to deliver an assessment of Russia's Artificial Intelligence capabilities. To determine their current state of research and deployment of the technology in their military, intelligence and commercial sectors, research was conducted using Open Source Intelligence (OSINT).

A. *Russia will continue to improve its Artificial Intelligence knowledge*

Russia, as one of the top three superpowers is a relatively recent national level player in the development of Artificial Intelligence (AI). Russia is increasing their scientific and academic communities' focus on AI development. Their strategy is to establish and strengthen relationships with U.S. AI research universities, academics and commercial entities who are advancing the science and practical use of AI. Using this collaborative approach, it is almost certain Russia will continue to advance its Artificial Intelligence knowledge.

To rally support of the Russian people, in September of 2017 Vladimir Putin repeated a quote from Lyndon B. Johnson made approximately 60 years before when, as the senate-majority leader, Johnson predicted the dawning of a revolutionary new technological era when he discussed the importance of reaching into outer space in the Senate Armed Service Committee's Preparedness Subcommittee by saying "Control of space means control of the world" (Wasser, 2005). At the time, the race to launch satellites and people into space was a top priority for society. It was believed that the successful pursuit of this scientific goal would impact society in a profound way. When talking about artificial intelligence during a speech in 2017, Putin said, "Whoever becomes the leader in this sphere will become the ruler of the world" (Allen-Husain, 2017).

Putin's statement may be rather hyperbolic however, like the moment in Johnson's era, it is widely accepted that Artificial Intelligence (AI) will have a profound impact on society. For AI, it will not only impact society as the space race did, but since it includes improving our understanding of how thought works, it will expand the knowledge of humanity. Along with an increasing our self-awareness there are many ideas, both in the scientific and social community, how artificial intelligence will evolve to positively impact society. The mutual agreement amongst those who understand AI is that a society who doesn't embrace AI now will later be consumed by those who have committed today.

Along with possessing two of the three most powerful militaries, both the U.S. and China are current leaders in Artificial Intelligence (AI). However, Russia, the remaining member of the top powers triumvirate currently comes in at a very distant third with their AI research and development efforts. Their ranking is based on the total financial investments made by government and non-government sources in research and development (Jacobsen, 2018). The numbers for Russia are much smaller since they have only recently made a serious commitment to AI research and development (Woody-Cheng, 2018). Though Russia has only recently jumped on the superpower AI bandwagon, their central government is making up for lost time by actively backing their scientific and academic communities by making strong commitments of financial and political capital for AI research. Also, they are aggressively pursuing opportunities to incorporate AI into their militaries and intelligence services.

To support a national effort to increase the knowledge of AI and to determine practical uses for it, in 2012 Vladimir Putin began the process to create the Russian Foundation for Advanced Research Projects (*Фонд перспективных исследований*) also known as the Foundation for Advanced Studies (FAS). His Presidential decree initiated the process to first gain acceptance then later secure financing from the Russian Parliament. Like the U.S.' Defense Advanced Research Projects Agency (DARPA), the Russia's FAS is committed to research and development of technology to improve their country's defenses. In the context of AI, the leadership of Russia wants to advance the use of Artificial intelligence in the military.

Since Putin's 2017 Homeric statement about the leader of AI ruling the world, Russia has begun aggressively undertaking AI research and development in several parts of their society, especially the military. Along with the focus on delivering AI to the battlefield, there is a burgeoning effort amongst Russia's political leadership, scholars, and scientists to advance their knowledge of AI. For example, Russia is establishing a center for AI development in their country. In February of this year, the Kremlin displayed an architectural mockup of a technology center, dubbed ERA. The center will be in the Moscow area and it is dedicated to scientific research and development, with its "main goal" of the "creation of military artificial intelligence" (President of Russia, 2018).

To help focus their effort, in March of this year, the Russian Ministry of Defense, along with their Academy of Sciences and Ministry of Education, held a conference to define a national strategy for how Russia should proceed to grow their Artificial Intelligence capabilities. From the conference, they developed a 10-point plan that encouraged these agencies to work together to "create and implement artificial intelligence technologies" (MOD-AI, 2018). Appendix B contains an English translation of the conference's plenary list with recommended next steps. Certain key points from the forum's document should be noted:

Point 4: The Ministry Of Defense (MOD), Federal Agency for Scientific Organizations, (Lomonosov)Moscow State University, and FITS IU RAS (Federal Research Center, Informatics and Management of the Russian Academy of Sciences) will work together to create a laboratory for research and testing of Artificial Intelligence technologies. The center, VIT ERA is also known as a Technopolis (MOD-AI, 2018).

Point 5: This paragraph instructs the Russian Academy of Sciences and Advanced Research Foundation to create a "National Center for Artificial Intelligence" The center will focus on designing and implementing an infrastructure that will support scientific development of artificial intelligence. This is a call for technology architects to create an environment that will support scientific development in artificial intelligence and provide one where practical use for AI can be researched (MOD-AI, 2018).

This is an important point since a challenge, at this time, is that artificial intelligence development is heavily buried in the scientific community, with limited participation from technology Architects. Good technology Architects can bridge the scientific theories into sound business models. While governments and commercial organizations of the U.S. and China are, almost exclusively, investing in

Scientists to develop new of AI algorithms, cognitive functions and computing hardware, investment in Architects to integrate AI into existing and new environments is almost non-existent in nations working on AI. However, this is not true for Russia, they are focusing more attention on AI architecture and implementation than scientific breakthroughs which means they may field AI solutions quicker than their adversaries.

Point 6: This point directs the MOD, Ministry of Education and Science, and the Russian Academy of Sciences to monitor and research AI developments occurring in other countries. It is this point that encourages the gathering of intellectual knowledge from other countries (MOD-IMTF, 2017). In a not so subtle way, this point encourages the "acquisition" of information from non-Russian entities and especially those that are allied with Russia.

Point 7: This section is an important tie in to the militarization of AI since it requires the MOD to "conduct a series of military games" ..." with the definition of the influence of artificial intelligence model" (MOD-AI, 2018). The various levels of warfare, such as strategic, operational and tactical must be incorporated into the gaming exercises.

Russia is moving quickly to fulfill the work laid out in their national AI forum and to raise their level of sophistication in AI. While their direct investment in AI pales to those made by the U.S. and China (Bendett, 2018) they are quickly building a sound foundation for AI to be integrated into their military infrastructure. Along with Russia's central government starting to invest more in AI research, the global academic community, especially

American institutions, have also been partnering with Russian scientists on AI. For example, The Massachusetts Institute of Technology (MIT) created the Skolkovo Institute of Technology in Moscow. The institute is focused on six categories of scientific knowledge, one being Artificial Intelligence. (*https://www.masterstudies.com/universities/Russia/The-Skolkovo-Institute-of-Science-and-Technology-(Skoltech)/*). This relationship with MIT has provided access for Russian scientists to some of the leading scientists in AI development. This relationship has not yet produced any recognized AI research from Russia.

As to their intellectual capability as a nation, Russia has a long history of commitment to education and fully supports science and engineering. Along with a priority on education, they have embraced technology and the global Internet. Evidence of their commitment to education reveals that Russia possess a "literacy rate of 99% and nearly 70% enrolled in post-secondary education. As for online technology, Russia boasts the largest Internet market in Europe, with 59.7 million users, and an astounding 230.5 million mobile phones" (Wharton-Skolkovo, 2013).

Their strong participation in the Internet has exposed them to many different nations' technical infrastructures and the cultures of those nations. This exposure helps them better understand those they consider their friends and those who are their adversaries. As a result, they have awareness of the social norms and values of select other nations, such as the U.S.. Understanding of another culture is very helpful in an Information Warfare campaign.

Russia, like many other nations on the Internet, can easily acquire information on topics like scientific discoveries in Artificial Intelligence. In addition, by using the Internet, Russia can view another countries' political parties and come to understand their strengths and vulnerabilities. They develop these profiles by examining what a political party and its opposing parties post online about each other. Also collected and studied is what citizens are saying about the parties, its candidates and leadership in social media and political discussion web sites.

In addition to searching for social information, the Internet makes it easier to communicate with other nation's citizens, scientists, and engineers, especially those in a highly connected society such like the United States. For example, Russia can acquire AI knowledge by simply studying the scholarly papers published by leading scientists, architects and engineers in the field of AI, then further communicate with them through Email and Social Media sites. All this technical reconnaissance and collaboration with the citizens of an adversary nation can be done while sitting comfortably in an apartment in St. Petersburg, beside the Baltic Sea. This is all possible since the people in scientific and technical disciplines encourage the sharing of knowledge by publicly publishing their work and make themselves available to others interested in their research. In many cases these scientists and scholars are required to routinely publish and represent their research as a requirement of academic tenure.

The Internet makes it easy to deliver information and it increases the opportunity to exploit those that are eager to please, naïve or want to hedge their bets by allying themselves with both sides of adversarial relationships. It is this latter type of behavior, of someone or a nation playing both sides, that is presents a great risk, since the person sitting in the middle may knowingly or be unaware, they are being used as a "conduit" for intelligence to flow between adversaries.

In addition to Russia being able to harvest knowledge from academic and scientific relationships, their close relationship with India provides them a country they can use or partner with to enable India to become a conduit country to gather intelligence about American corporate Artificial Intelligence work. India is in possession of American data, designs and operational information as a result of India's widespread presence in American IT.

Some of the U.S. companies that use Indian labor extensively are the ones developing and implementing artificial intelligence, such as Google, Amazon, IBM and NVIDIA. In addition, India has many citizens attending American academic institutions where American professors and scholars are developing AI technology, like Carnegie Mellon University, Massachusetts Institute of Technology, Stanford University and several other American research universities.

"The India-Russia bilateral relationship has a long history and a broad international context" (Godbole, 2018). The Russian-Indian relationship referred to as *Российско-индийские отношения* in Russia and भारत-रूस सम्बन्ध in India, is one that was especially strong during the Cold War-Soviet era, with the saying "Hindi Rusi bhai-bhai (Indians and Russians are brothers)" (Pande-Thoburn, 2016). It waned slightly in the first decade of the 21st century and is now showing signs of returning to its former, Soviet era strength. The relationship was reaffirmed this year when India's Prime Minister Modi and Russia's President Vladimir Putin met May 21st in Sochi Russia. "PM Modi said India and Russia have been friends for a long time" and President Putin said "Russia and India maintain a high strategic level of partnership, close cooperation between the two countries' defense ministries" (Times of India, 2018). Before the meeting of Modi and Putin, Indian officials were asked if they were concerned about sanctions being imposed on them by America because they violated the U.S. Countering America's Adversaries Through Sanctions Act (CAATSA) by committing to a large weapons purchase from Russia, the Indian officials responded by saying "India is not going to allow its defence engagement with Russia to be dictated by any other country" (Times of India, 2018).

In addition to India purchasing most of their weapons from Russia, other evidence of their close relationship to Russia is their ongoing joint military development projects. For example, India and Russia's partners on the BrahMos I and BrahMos II Hypersonic missiles. India co-designed the missile with Russia who is marketing the weapon. They are also jointly working on a newer version of a missile known as the BrahMos-A, which is an air launched supersonic missile that can travel close to Mach 3 and reach a range of 290 Kilometers (ET Bureau, 2018). The intent is to increase the missile's speed up to a Hypersonic rate, which is Mach 5 or greater (Mach 5=3,836 MPH)(ET Bureau, 2018). Hypersonic missiles pose a great risk since currently there are no missile defense systems that can defend against objects traveling at such a high rate of speed (Gregg, 2018).

B. *Russia will increase the use of Artificial Intelligence in their kinetic weapons*

It appears Russia's primary interest in AI is to find ways that the technology can enhance their military capabilities. For some of their kinetic weapons they are already incorporating elements of AI, such as Machine Learning (ML), Artificial Neural Networking (ANN) and a Convolutional Neural Network (ConvNet) to enhance weapons that are completely controlled by humans and in those that are semi-autonomous. Russia is also developing AI supported full-autonomous military weapons, however the delivery of such weapons will take them longer and they appear to still be in a research phase of development.

Russia is actively working to incorporate AI into their kinetic weapons and are making progress. Even though most of their current and near-term AI architectures are focused on image recognition systems, it is almost certain they will continue to increase their use of AI in their kinetic weapons and expand their capabilities.

By incorporating artificial intelligence into weapons system, it is hoped the war fighter will have a better chance of survival, able to fight more effectively, and cause less collateral damage from a fight. Other important benefits of AI are that it can operate for longer periods than humans, not degrade in performance due to fatigue and tolerate inhospitable environments. Also, AI systems can possess greater sensory accuracy (vision and audio), process more information and at a faster rate than humans.

An example of Russia using AI to assist humans to control weapons is the use of it in their Sukhoi Su-35(**Сухой Су-**

35) aircraft. The fighter jet has an AI coordinated target acquisition, analysis and weapon response system that can identify and track multiple targets simultaneously (Defense World, 2017). A similar system is deployed in their stealthy Sukhoi Su-57 fighter (**Сухой Су**-57)(Sputnik-1, 2018). In addition, it is expected their upcoming Mikoyan MiG-35 (**Микоян МиГ**-35) fighter will also have AI capabilities (Allen-Husain, 2017). At a minimum it is expected the new Mikoyan fighter will have the same AI assisted targeting system as the Sukhoi aircrafts.

Along with AI integration into their aircraft, they are also working to AI enable Unmanned Combat Ground Vehicles (UCGV). An example of an AI assisted UCGV is their Nerekhta combat robot (Atherton-Weapons, 2018) which is a remotely controlled, tank-like, semi-autonomous UCGV that fights alongside soldiers in the field using AI. In addition to aerial and ground vehicles, they are also perfecting stationary weapons such as a turret based high-power machine guns that is assisted by AI. One such turret utilizes an onboard ANN assisted image recognition system to help discern targets (Bedard, 2017). The weapon is designed and built by one of Russia's primary weapons manufacturers, the Kalashnikov Concern (***Концерн Калашникова***). They have made it clear they intend to develop AI controlled weapons by stating: "In the nearest future we plan to unveil a whole line of neural network-based products" (Miley, 2017).

It appears Russia's primary AI technology for their Lethal Autonomous Weapons Systems (LAWS), is image recognition, which is consistent with most of their AI solutions seen in their country's civilian and intelligence sector. For example, a successful image recognition application called Find Face (*https://findface.ru/*) uses facial recognition to harvest social media sites for a person's information using a single picture of them. The application was originally developed by Atrem Kukharenko, Alexander Kabakov and Maxim Perlin of Ntech Lab Ltd. Originally, they provided public access to their application as a service. The service worked by someone simply uploading a picture to the service's user site then it would search the Russian Social Media site "Vkontakte's 200 million users, FindFace's algorithm is able to search through a database of over one billion photographs in mere seconds, using only four standard servers" (Burgett, 2016). The core application could also be used against other social media sites since it did not require integration with a targeted Social Media site's Application Programming Interface (API). Since its introduction, the application's availability for civilian use has been restricted by the Russian government. Due to the benefit of the tool, it is believed that the Russian government has exercised its right to "obtain sensitive technical information from industry" (NCSC, 2018) and also shut down general access to the application.

The reason Russia appears farther along in the integration of AI image recognition is due to their study of the considerable research and development that has already been done by other countries' scientists in this field. The preponderance of research in image recognition comes from the U.S. The breakthrough, which became the practical basis for current image recognition, was made by a pair of scientists in the 1950s, David Hubel and Torsten Wiesel while collaborating and John Hopkins University. They discovered how animals processed images using a 3-Dimensional array that included neurons related to the visual cortex (Fehlhaber, 2014).

Their breakthrough is the foundational science behind the optimal type of 3-Dimensional ANN that is used for image processing known as a Convolutional Neural Network or ConvNet. We now see the use of a ConvNet in practically all systems that use image recognition such as the facial recognition systems being used in airports around the country like those deployed by the Department of Homeland Security (Aratani, 2018) and in consumer drones (Dronelli, 2017) that have human tracking capabilities.

In the currently evolving next generation battlefield there will be fully autonomous AI controlled Unmanned Combat Vehicles that can operate independently to complete a mission. These systems are being developed by the U.S and it is reported these systems are also being developed by Russia. In 2015 it was revealed Russia was working on a new UCUV (Unmanned Combat Underwater Vehicle) "nuclear powered undersea drone designed to carry an enormous thermonuclear warhead" (Geist-Lohn, 2018). The autonomous undersea drone is known as the Status-6 and will be controlled by an onboard ANN, which makes it an "AI on the edge" device, meaning the device has its own on-board Neural Network so it doesn't have to communicate to an external cognitive system. This is important since bidirectional communications is required to control a drone and reliable communication between this drone and an external operator cannot occur due to the radio frequency absorption of water. The inability to communicate between the operator and a UCUV is even worse if circumnavigation of the Earth occurs through glacial polar regions. For underwater drones AI on the edge will be key since even the newer communications technologies, like TARF (Translational Acoustic RF) proposed by Francesco Tonolini and Fadel Abid of MIT, is only unidirectional with the signal only going outbound from the drone (Atherton-TARF, 2018).

C. Russia will incorporate AI to fully assist in command and control systems:

The modern theater of war requires a decision support system that is an intelligent grid that comprises systems for Command, Control, Communications, Computers, Intelligence, Surveillance, and Reconnaissance(C4ISR)(Starr, n.d.). By using the assistive nature of AI, such a decision support system can be enhanced by an ANN that can accept information from many sources, place it into a central aggregation point, quickly analyze the information, and present the results of its analysis to commanders.

The sources of the information must come from both the kinetic and the Cyber battlefield. The information that is fed into the central aggregator can be rapidly analyzed using discriminative cognitive analysis to identify enemy patterns of activity that would not be detected by traditional discrete analysis of battlefields. Even though this is a simplistic example and only one of many possible AI enhancements for military intelligence analysis, it will still aid with higher quality decision making. This is also a current state model of the AI analytic process, over time as the aggregated data increases in its quantity of data points and AI powered predictive analytics continues to evolve, so will the quality of intelligence being provide to strategic and tactical warfare commanders. Over time AI evolve to bring leaders closer to the point of Prescriptive

Analytics, whereby the outcome of a specific action is known in advance (Appendix D).

Along with fielding robotic systems like Unmanned Combat Vehicles, Russia is also fielding military command and control systems that contain some form of artificial intelligence, but it appears they are only focusing on the kinetic battlefield. It is probable they will expand their AI based C2 systems to include both the Cyber and kinetic battlefields.

An example of their kinetic battlefield AI based C2 system is their Polyana-D4M1 command and control (C2) mobile post that is used for battlefield air defense (Sputknik-2, 2017). The Polyana-D4M1 began its life in the mid-1980s and has been upgraded several times to its current state and it is reported to now have some AI capabilities. The C2 system deploys close to an active battlefield and appears to have similar AI capabilities of other Russian military systems, which is a targeting assistance system, based on AI image recognition. The system also appears to have a complimentary Threat Management (TM) system, although the level of sophistication of its neural network cannot be assessed using only OSINT.

The Polyana-D4M1 can monitor air traffic in an 800x800 square kilometer radius, simultaneously monitor 500 enemy objects, and actively track approximately half of them. The wide area view is a result of being able to collect information from ground and air radars and Air Traffic Control (ATC) centers. The complete system has multiple self-propelled vehicles which include the core aggregator system (which also the Command staff vehicle), a support vehicle and two power generation systems. Not only can the system aggregate information from subordinate radars, ATC centers, command posts and headquarters but it can be a command center to initiate attack while it simultaneously collects and consolidates battlefield information to provide command level intelligence.

The Polyana-D4M1 command center can operate in a passive manner by only 'responding' to a human commander. Next, it can act in a consultative manner by offering recommendations based on the results of its discriminative analysis of the data provided to it by its subordinate systems. It is speculated the recommendations the system offers will be drawn from a selection of pre-defined options that match the findings of its discriminative analysis. Finally, the Polyana-D4M1 can work in a fully autonomous mode. When fully autonomous, the manufacturer states Artificial Intelligence will be used and the "operator does not take part in the control process" (Sputnik-2, 2017). No specifics of what form of AI will be used, nor the training the AI neural network has undergone. Most importantly, it is unknown what loss of control the operator loses in when the system is operating in the fully autonomous mode.

D. *Russia will independently develop AI assisted Cyber and Information Warfare systems*

Along with Russia's efforts to continue to incorporate AI into their kinetic weapons and command and control systems, Russia also intends to enhance their AI Cyber and Information Warfare (IW) capabilities. Russia is skilled at conducting IW campaigns using their corral of human Trolls, weak minded and greedy people to conduct social media and traditional media attack campaigns. Despite their independent IW ability, they are dependent on other nations for Cyber weapons, but they have proven they can modify and deploy the weapons successfully. But they have not presented a unique Cyber weapon that exploits a previously unknown vulnerability. This latter ability is known as the "Zero Day" test in the hacker community and it is considered a good qualification of someone's "skillz"(*https://www.urbandictionary.com/define.php?term=skillz*).

At the core of the upcoming next generation of Cyber and Information Warfare will be Quantum Computing based Artificial Intelligence (QC-AI). When viewing their current capabilities in computer system research and their lack of advanced Cyber security development, it is believed they will probably not be able to independently develop the next generation of Artificial Intelligence based Cyber Weapons.

Russia has shown a willingness to conduct direct Cyber-attacks against foreign targets. For example, their Cyber-attacks against the Ukraine where Russian Cyber fighters have negatively impacted parts of the Ukrainian power grid using Cyber weapons. Both attacks occurred during the Christmas season. The first attack, in December of 2015 was manually initiated, whereas the second attack, a year later during Christmas 2016, was more automated. (Sebenius, 2017). The attack was more than a nuisance attack since it risked lives due to it being launched during the winter season in Ukraine when temperatures are very low.

Russia also engages in cross-border IW attacks. In fact, "For more than a century, Russia has relied on disinformation, propaganda and other similar measures to achieve its objectives. For the last three decades, it has exploited its growing capabilities in Cyberspace to spy on, influence and punish others" (McClintock, n.d.). Finally given Russia's 59.7 million Internet users, it means they have a well-connected society that could be easily called up to support their nation in a Cyberwar which they appear to have done in some capacity during their IW attack on the U.S. 2016 Presidential election.

The Russian government and its intelligence services use of contractors and allied nations makes it difficult to accurately assess the true capabilities of its Russian government versus that of third parties. For example, the Advanced Persistent Groups (APT) APT-28 (Fancy Bear/Sofacy), APT-29 (Cozy Bear) and Guccifer 2.0 are not formally GRU's (*Glavnoye Razvedyvatel'noye Upravleniye*) employees (Carroll, 2016) but are independent groups overseen by the GRU. Most of Russia's hacking groups are primarily located in and around St. Petersburg, Russia. While these groups are presented as independent groups by the Russian government, it is not realistic to believe they are independent since any developed nation, especially one with a very controlling government, would allow a computer hacking group to operate independently in their nation without some form of oversight, especially ones that conducts nation level attacks.

In the Cyber security world Russia is not thought to be a creator of Cyber weapons, but rather an acquirer and embolden user of them. In fact, they are very good at acquiring tools and technology through honest, dishonest and illegal means. It should be noted that the term 'honest' carries a loose ethical definition for Russians, especially when they are doing something they feel is in their nationalistic interest.

Along with good acquisition efforts, they have proven they are willing to combine the use of Cyber weapons with the IW skills they have developed over the decades to attack an adversary. The 2016 Presidential election was a good example of Russia's modern unconventional warfare capabilities since it paired Cyber-attacks with IW attacks. In this well-coordinated attack, Cyber weapons were used to harvest sensitive messages from a political party that was in opposition to the candidate they were supporting. The acquired material was then used in an IW social media and traditional media attack to smear the opposing candidate.

The attack, though not novel to certain European countries who have been victims of similar attacks by Russia-such as Estonia-was at a scale not seen before, since it involved the U.S. and its highest political office. Throughout the Cyber and IW attacks Russia maintained their self-stated innocence since the attack was not done by Russian government employees. True it was not done by Russian government employees' hands, but it was done by third party hacking groups that are compensated and overseen by Russian government and military intelligence services. While the Russian government maintained its innocence, data fingerprint evidence of a Russian country-based attack was found in the modifications made to the Cyber weapons used in the attacks. Using this hacking forensic analysis, attribution of the Cyber-attack was made to the GRU's APT-28, APT-29, and Guccifer 2.0 (Carroll, 2016). Even Julian Assange, a close friend of Russia, aided Putin and his allies in the offensive by posting the captured Emails from the Cyber offensive on his WikiLeaks site.

How Russia conducted the attack on the 2016 Presidential election serves not only as a qualifier of Russia's capabilities in the new technological and information age battlefield, but evidences that it is important for commanders leading in the new battlefield to have a mature strategy that includes Cyber and Information Warfare. It should be noted that most attention is paid to the tools and techniques used in Cyber-attacks, which is very important, however more important it is the material acquired from Cyber-attacks. The material is the valuable part of the intelligence that feeds the IW component of Hybrid Warfare.

Russia appears to understand that coordination of the Cyber and IW battlefield will continue to rise in importance as development and deployment of computer-controlled weapons are initiated for the battlefield. This means that just having the newest technology does not guarantee success, especially if technology is sent into battle by people who don't understand it or know how to deploy it effectively. The truism, 'Just because you give a man a shield, does not make him a warrior'(*Plato*) is important, especially in the Cyber and Information Warfare component of Hybrid Warfare. History has shown that even an Army that has the best weapons are not guaranteed success on the battlefield, especially if leaders don't update their strategy and tactics to match the new weapons.

The commercial sector is quickly advancing how to teach AI systems while improving artificial systems' cognitive abilities. For example, Deep Learning (DL), one of the important tools for teaching AI, is well understood and increasingly effective, as are other methods to teach AI such as Reinforcement Learning (RL). The level of cognitive ability of the AI system after DL or RL training is directly related to the quantity and quality of information contained in the training material, known as training sets. Unfortunately, DL and RL learning is slow and in the case of DL, large training sets are required. Though RL is not as dependent on large amounts of data to effectively train, it still requires a quality training set to seed the learning process and is slow like DL training.

Training set data acquisition by Russia will be possible, although tougher than sharing or buying Cyber tools. This is due to training sets coming from large datasets that are costlier to create since it requires a lot of input, time and physical storage space. In addition, unlike Cyber tools and IW Trolls, large datasets are harder to move around due to their file(s) sizes. Moving large amounts of data, or this type of data, is more apt to be detected by data security monitoring systems. These additional challenges of acquiring valuable training datasets can be overcome if Russia works with once their conduit countries that have access to this data because of their mutual relationships with the U.S. and Russia.

Since it is tough to move large sets of data needed for proper training of an AI system, alternative methods of training will be explored by Russia, such as creating Generative Adversarial Networks (GAN) (*https://papers.nips.cc/paper/5423-generative-adversarial-nets.pdf*) (Appendix C) to enable and AI system to train itself. GANs can be much faster at training a system since it uses an AI system to teach another AI system. Along with being a faster and automated training method, a

GAN eliminates the need to acquire a large, cumbersome amount of data. While a GAN based training, system is not hard to understand or construct, the challenging part is to know how to setup right GAN to properly teach the target AI system.

In addition to GANs for improving learning, GANs are also being explored to thwart computer systems and systems that protect them, including AI based protection systems. An example of one type of GAN used for illicit purposes is a Malicious Generative Adversarial Networks (MalGANs) which can automatically, and in a few iterative attempts, successfully deliver malicious software to Email recipients that are protected by Firewalls and malware software detectors. One type of GAN, a 2-dimensional, works by repeatedly attempting delivery and monitoring the failed attempts, then maps out the security profile of the target defending system and creates an attack vector that will successfully bypass detection. In a more sophisticated GAN, referred to as a 3-dimensional GAN, a detector can be used on the far side of the targeted system and offer feed back to the GAN. The advantage of the 3-dimensional GAN is that learning the targeted system will be done much faster and in a such a manner that raises less suspicion of itself, since a 2-dimensional GAN tends to create a lot of "noise" of itself.

In fact, even if the target environment is protected by an AI based malware detection system, a MalGAN may eventually defeat it. For a primer on GANs and MalGANs see Appendix C. One way to attack an AI defense system and render it ineffective is to use a GAN is to corrupt the cognitive abilities of the AI defense system by re-teaching it. Therefore, to prevent an AI system from being defeated, its cognitive function must be protected against corruption. While the preceding is was one approach to 'kill' and 'protect' AI systems, there are other techniques.

Despite Russia's current appearance of limited GAN abilities, there is interest by some of their scholars in this field. For example, Anton Karazeev, a research fellow at the Russian Quantum (computing) Center in Moscow, is a respected GAN researcher and maintains a Website where openly shares his ideas on GANs: (*https://blog.statsbot.co/generative-adversarial-networks-gans-engine-and-applications-f96291965b47*).

The next step in AI's evolution will involve pairing artificial intelligence with Quantum Computing (QC). What makes QC so attractive for AI is that it can perform more complex AI tasks much quicker, especially those that require simultaneous using 3-Dimensional Neural Networking that is currently done by a ConvNet. Early practical testing and international collaboration on QC has centered on secure communications systems. Some of the testing occurring of QC based communications systems are focused on using QC to decipher encrypted communications using the simultaneous computing capability of QC (Mavroeidis, Kamer, et. al) and the exploitation of Quantum Entanglement for simultaneous communication across long distances (Lerner, 2018).

It is critical for national governments that have the intellectual and financial capability to properly support QC development do so by investing in and protecting their nation's companies and individuals' intellectual rights in the areas of QC they are developing. The recent signing into law of the NQIA (National Quantum Initiative Act, 2018) that contained $1.2+ Billion dollars' worth of funding for Quantum research is a good start to help keep with other nations like Russia who understand the importance of this technology and are making investments in the science and committing resources.   In addition to supporting development in their nation, and with the other nations they are collaborating with, Russia can also acquire the knowledge and systems required to have their own QC environments by using one of their conduit countries who have access to QC systems of an organizations they have a relationship with.

Currently QC based AI is still in an early stage of development however there have been some recent breakthroughs to help build the foundation for AC-AI. For example, a company in California, Rigetti Computing, has built the prototype of a QC processor (Knight, 2017) that can conduct discriminative analysis on datasets to identify patterns, which is a common capability of AI based Machine Learning. An even more promising demonstration of merging AI into QC is a technique by Francesco Tacchino and his colleagues at the Italian University of Pavia. Tacchino and his team successfully created an Artificial Neuron (AN), known traditionally as a perceptron, which is the basic building block of an ANN. They created the perceptron and validated it on IBM's Q-5 processor (MIT, 2018).

Russia has an appearance of getting involved in QC with what they refer to as their Deep Quantum Labs that is located at their Skolkovo center (Leskov,2011), but there is no evidence in the scientific community they are producing worthwhile QC research. But there are well respected Russian born scientists involved, so it is possible the center may eventually be recognized for their theoretical quantum research. Along with trying to bring international scientists to the research centers they are funding, they are actively reaching out with funding and resource commitments to other countries involved in QC research and development. An example of Russia committing resources is the recent success of a secure communications test ran by the Italian Space Agency using satellites from the Russian Global Navigation Satellite System GLONASS (Globalnaya Navigazionnaya Sputnikovaya Sistema) (Institute of Physics, 2018).

ACRONYMS

ACRONYMS
AI=Artificial Intelligence
AN=Artificial Neuron
ANN=Artificial Neural Network
API=Application Programming Interface
ATC=Air Traffic Control
BN=Biological Neuron
BNN=Biological Neural Network
C2=Command and Control
C4ISR= Command, Control, Communications, Computers and Intelligence, Surveillance, and Reconnaissance
CAATSA=Countering America's Adversaries Through Sanctions Act
ConvNet= Convolutional Neural Network
CPU=Central Processing Unit
DL=Deep Learning
DHS=Department of Homeland Security
DL=Deep Learning
DNN=Deep Neural Networks (also known as Stacked Neural Networks)
FAS= Foundation for Advanced Studies
GAN=Generative Adversarial Network
GLONASS=Globalnaya Navigazionnaya Sputnikovaya Sistema
GPU=Graphics Processing Unit
IW=Information Warfare
LAWS=Lethal Autonomous Weapons Systems
MalGAN=Malicious Generative Adversarial Network
MIT= Massachusetts Institute of Technology
ML=Machine Learning
NIE=National Intelligence Estimate
NQIA=National Quantum Initiative Act

NSF=National Science Foundation
NSFNet=National Science Foundation Network
NNP=Network Neural Processor
NPU=Neural Processing Unit
OSINT=Open Source Intelligence
PLC=Programmable Logic Controllers
QC-AI=Quantum Computing based Artificial
Intelligence
RL= Reinforcement Learning
TM=Threat Management
TPU=Tensor Processing Unit
UCV=Unmanned Combat Vehicle
UCAV=Unmanned Combat Aerial Vehicles
UCGV=Unmanned Combat Ground Vehicle
UCUV=Unmanned Combat Underwater Vehicle

BIBLIOGRAPHY

CIA (2008, July 07). "Words of Estimative Probability". Central Intelligence Agency. Retrieved from: https://www.cia.gov/library/center-for-the-study-of-intelligence/csi-publications/books-and-monographs/sherman-kent-and-the-board-of-national-estimates-collected-essays/6words.html

Wasser, A. (2005, June 26). "LBJ's Space Race: What We Didn't Know Then". The Space Settlement Institute. Retrieved from: http://www.space-settlement-institute.org/Articles/LBJSpaceRaceHistory.pdf

Allen, J., Husain, A. (2017, November 3). "The Next Space Race is Artificial Intelligence". Foreign Policy. Retrieved from: https://foreignpolicy.com/2017/11/03/the-next-space-race-is-artificial-intelligence-and-america-is-losing-to-china/

Jacobsen, B. (2018, January 8). "5 Countries Leading the way in AI". Future Platforms. Retrieved from: https://www.futuresplatform.com/blog/5-countries-leading-way-ai-artificial-intelligence-machine-learning

Woody,C.,Cheng,J. (2018, March 1). "Here's the hardware the world's top 25 militaries have in their arsenal". Business Insider. Retrieved from: https://www.businessinsider.com/here-are-the-worlds-most-powerful-militaries-2018-2

President of Russia (2018, February 23). "Presentation of Era innovation technopolis". Retrieved from: http://en.kremlin.ru/events/president/news/56923

BIBLIOGRAPHY *(cont.)*

MOD-IMTF (2017, June 2017). "International Military-Technical Forum. General Information". Ministry of Defence of The Russian Federation. Retrieved from: http://www.rusarmyexpo.com/army2018/general_infor mation

MOD-AI (2018). "Conference Artificial Intelligence: Problems and Solutions -2018". Ministry of Defence of the Russian Federation Retrieved from: http://mil.ru/conferences/is-intellekt.htm

Bendett, S. (2018, April 4). "In AI, Russia Is Hustling to Catch Up". DefenseOne. Retrieved from: https://www.defenseone.com/ideas/2018/04/russia-races-forward-ai-development/147178/

Wharton- Skolkovo (2013, December 20). "Skolkovo: A Case Study in Government-supported innovation". Knowledge at Wharton. Retrieved from: http://knowledge.wharton.upenn.edu/article/skolkovo-case-study-government-supported-innovation/

Godbole, S. (2018, July 2). "Future of the India-Russia relationship post Sochi summit". Brookings Institution. Retrieved from: https://www.brookings.edu/blog/up-front/2018/07/02/future-of-the-india-russia-relationship-post-sochi-summit/

Pande,A., Thoburn, H. (2016, December 16). "Why the India-Russia Relationship Works". The Diplomat. Retrieved from: https://thediplomat.com/2016/12/why-the-india-russia-relationship-works/

BIBLIOGRAPHY *(cont.)*

Times of India (2018, May 21). "PM Modi, Russia President Putin hold 'extremely productive' talks on bilateral, global issues". Retrieved from: https://timesofindia.indiatimes.com/india/pm-modi-meets-russian-president-putin-for-first-informal-summit/articleshow/64258645.cms

ET Bureau (2018, July 14). "India successfully test-fires BrahMos from Sukhoi-30 fighter aircraft". The Economic Times. Retrieved from: https://economictimes.indiatimes.com/news/defence/india-successfully-test-fires-brahmos-from-sukhoi-30-fighter-aircraft/articleshow/61751675.cms

Gregg, A. (2018, April 18). "Air Force awards massive hypersonic weapon contract to Lockheed Martin. The Washington Post. Retrieved from: https://www.washingtonpost.com/news/business/wp/2018/04/18/air-force-awards-massive-hypersonic-weapon-contract-to-lockheed-martin/?noredirect=on&utm_term=.6e74cd98822f

Defense World (2017, November 13). "Russian Su-35 Fighter Equipped With 'Artificial Intelligence'. Defense World. Retrieved from: http://www.defenseworld.net/news/21257/Russian_Su_35_Fighter_Equipped_With__Artificial_Intelligence_#.W_HXbOhKhhE

Sputnik-1 (2018, August 24). "Russian Fifth-Gen Stealth Fighter to Get Artificial Intelligence-Source". Sputnik News. Retrieved from: https://sputniknews.com/russia/201808241067430359-russia-su-57-fighter-jet-gets-ai/

Atherton-Weapons. Atherton, K. (2018, June 11). "Russia prepares for a future of making autonomous weapons". C4ISRNET. Retrieved from: https://www.c4isrnet.com/electronic-warfare/2018/06/11/russia-prepares-for-a-future-of-making-autonomous-weapons/

Bedard, P. (2017, July 17). "The maker of the AK-47 made a robotic, AI gun system for Russia". Business Insider. Retrieved from: https://www.businessinsider.com/the-maker-ak-47-made-robotic-ai-gun-system-for-russia-2017-7

Miley, J. (2017, July 14). "Russian Army Manufacturer Kalashnikov Develops Fully-Automated Killer Robots". Interesting Engineering. Retrieved from: https://interestingengineering.com/russian-kalashnikov-develops-fully-automated-killer-robots

Burgett, G. (2016, May 18). "FindFace is a new facial recognition app that could end public privacy". Digital Trends. Retrieved from: https://www.digitaltrends.com/photography/findface-social-networks-detect-people-public-with-70-reliability/

NCSC (2018). "Foreign Economic Espionage in Cyberspace". National Counterintelligence and Security Center. Retrieved from: https://www.dni.gov/files/NCSC/documents/news/20180724-economic-espionage-pub.pdf

Fehlhaber,K.(2014, October 29). Hubel and Wiesel $ the Neural Basis of Visual Perception. Knowing Neurons. Retrieved from: https://knowingneurons.com/2014/10/29/hubel-and-wiesel-the-neural-basis-of-visual-perception/

Aratani, L. (2018, September 15). "Facial-recognition scanners at airports raise privacy concerns". The Washington Post. Retrieved from: https://www.washingtonpost.com/local/trafficandcomm uting,/facial-recognition-scanners-at-airports-raise-privacy-concerns/2018/09/15/a312f6d0-abce-11e8-a8d7-0f63ab8b1370_story.html?utm_term=.7c0722c726d0

Dronelli, V. (2017, October 30). "THESE 4 DRONES CAN RECOGNIZE YOUR FACE. WHAT ARE THE BENEFITS OF THAT?". DRONESGLOBE. Retrieved from: http://www.dronesglobe.com/guide/face-recognition/

Geist, E., Lohn,A.J. (2018). "HOW MIGHT ARTIFICIAL INTELLIGENCE AFFECT THE RISK OF NUCLAR WAR". RAND Corporation. Retrieved from: https://www.rand.org/pubs/perspectives/PE296.html

Atherton-TARF. Atherton, K. (2018, August 28). "Is this the new wave of submerged communications?". C4ISRNET. Retrieved from: https://www.c4isrnet.com/c2-comms/2018/08/28/mit-discovers-way-for-submarines-to-talk-to-drones/

Starr, S.H. (n.d.). "C4ISR Assessment: Past, Present, and Future". International Command and Control Institute. Retrieved from: http://www.dodccrp.org/events/8th_ICCRTS/pdf/059.pdf

BIBLIOGRAPHY *(cont.)*

Sputknik-2 (2017, February 23). "Russia's Polyana Command & Control Post Can Track 500 Targets Simultaneously". Sputnik News. Retrieved from: https://sputniknews.com/military/201702231050980050-polyana-command-control-vehicle-info/

Sebenius, A. (2017, December 13). "Will Ukraine Be Hit by Yet Another Holiday Power-Grid Hack? Retrieved from: https://www.theatlantic.com/technology/archive/2017/12/ukraine-power-grid-hack/548285/

McClintock, B. (n.d.). "Russian Information Warfare: A Reality That Needs a Response'. RAND Corporation. Retrieved from: https://www.rand.org/blog/2017/07/russian-information-warfare-a-reality-that-needs-a.html

Carroll, L. (2016, July 31). "What we know about Russia's role in the DNC email leak". Politifact. Retrieved from: https://www.politifact.com/truth-o-meter/article/2016/jul/31/what-we-know-about-russias-role-dnc-email-leak/

Leskov, S. (2011, February 15). "A Quantum Center in Skolkovo". Russia Beyond. Retrieved from: https://www.rbth.com/articles/2011/02/15/a_quantum_center_in_skolkovo_12168

Mavroeidis,V.,Vishi,K.,Zych,M.D (2018). "The Impact of Quantum Computing on Present Cryptography". International Journal of Advance Computer Science and Applications. Retrieved from: https://arxiv.org/pdf/1804.00200.pdf

BIBLIOGRAPHY *(cont.)*

Lerner, L. (2018, October 24). "Quantum network to test unhackable communications". University of Chicago News. Retrieved from: https://news.uchicago.edu/story/quantum-network-test-unhackable-communications

National Quantum Initiative Act. H.R. 6227. House Report 115-950 (2018)

Knight, W. (2017, December 18). "A Startup Uses Quantum Computing to Boost Machine Learning". MIT Technology Review. Retrieved from: https://www.technologyreview.com/s/609804/a-startup-uses-quantum-computing-to-boost-machine-learning/

MIT (2018, November 16). "Machine learning meet quantum computing". MIT Technology Review. Retrieved from: https://www.technologyreview.com/s/612435/machine-learning-meet-quantum-computing/

Institute of Physics (2018, December 19). "Satellite study proves global quantum communication will be possible". Science X. Quantum Physics. Retrieved from: https://phys.org/news/2018-12-satellite-global-quantum.html

APPENDIX

Appendix A: Artificial Intelligence Technical Background

Appendix B: Russia Conference on "Artificial Intelligence: Problems and ways to solve them them-2018".

Appendix C: Generative Adversarial Network and MalGAN

Appendix D: Analytics Maturity Model

Appendix A

Artificial Intelligence Technical Background

The following is a reprint from the chapter "Technology Background" from the book "Artificial Intelligence Facial Recognition Threat Detection Environment (Artificial Intelligence Architectures)" by Mark Carey *(ISBN=9781727130393)*

Artificial Intelligence Conceptual View

The idea of Artificial Intelligence has been around for decades, but even longer in existence, is the human desire to codify what thought is and the laws that apply to it. For example, in the 4th Century B.C. Aristotle proposed a deductive scheme for thought and logic in his syllogism "common-sense rules about how we think" (Moral Robots, n.d.).

In less ancient times, during the 17th Century, Thomas Hobbes, author of the Leviathan, was famous for professing the notion of ratiocination, which is the process of "a reasoned train of thought" (*https://www.merriam-webster.com/dictionary/ratiocination*). He felt "thinking consists of symbolic operations" and that thoughts are "special brain tokens, which Hobbes called phantasms or thought parcels." (History-Computer, n.d.) This idea of a packetized thought processes is a foreshadowing of what we now call Neurons.

In the 1950s, scientist began to study how human though process functioned. Alan Turing suggested the concept of a "thinking" machine that could interact with humans. In 1952, Sir Alan Hodgkin and Sir Andrew Huxley proposed what is referred to as the Hodgkin-Huxley Model, which is a "model of the brain as neurons forming an electrical network, with individual neurons firing all-or-nothing (on/off) pulses." (Foote,2016). Then in 1956 the first open use of the term Artificial Intelligence came from the Dartmouth Summer Research Project on Artificial Intelligence conference which was organized by Dr. John McCarthy. Professor McCarthy, a Professor of mathematics at Dartmouth College, proposed at the conference that "...every aspect of learning or any other feature of intelligence can in principle be so precisely described that a machine can be made to simulate it" (Kapp,2006).

During the Cold War of the 1960s and 1970s, investments were made in AI research with much of it coming from the Defense Research Projects Agency (DARPA). (World-Information, n.d.). Unfortunately, the technology did not advance much during this period and it took until the 1980s for interest in AI to return with new efforts to develop and deliver AI, or "Expert Systems" as they were also known. (Foote,2016). In 1980, Digital Equipment Corporation (DEC) XCON system was an order entry system for the computer technology the company sold. XCON was designed to validate orders from DEC sales people using a rules-based approach to validate orders for missing or incorrect items. "At its peak, XCON had 2,500 rules...XCON was the first computer system to use AI techniques in solving real world problems" (Foote,2016). For a brief period in the late1980s until around the first part of 1993 interest in AI declined, led by the distraction of the rise of distributed computing known as the Personal Computer. However, as the 1990s progressed computer systems became more internetworked due to creation of the DARPANet that evolved into the NSFNet and finally the Internet.

Throughout the beginning of the 21st century, the distributed computing model has evolved into a centralized model, with large-scale computing centers housing an ever-increasing amount of data and processing power. These large-scale computing centers, or clouds as they are sometimes referred to, are managed by large organizations with dedicated teams supporting and selling their storage and compute capacity. The processing power contained in the computers that make up data centers has increased exponentially due to major advancements in microprocessor technology. In addition to increased computing power, there are now multiple options for microprocessor logic types that can be chosen based on the processing it will conduct. For example, the Graphics Processing Unit (GPU) Microprocessor which was originally designed to improve display graphics for visually intensive programs like Computer Generated Animation and Computer Games have been found to be superior to Central Processing Unit (CPU) Microprocessors for applications that are mathematically intensive such as Artificial Intelligence algorithms. (Wheeler, 2017)

Better than humanly possible, properly equipped computers can accept more input, store greater amounts of data, sort and recall it with greater speed and accuracy. Also, computers provide greater data resiliency with backup to other computers and long-term archive systems capable of storing data for decades. Since computers can input, output and manage data at a rate beyond the human capacity, complex data warehouse models have evolved to compliment human decision making. As a side effect of having the ability to store and process vast amounts of information, discovery of previously unknown patterns in data is occurring. This discovery of data patterns is important since it supports innovation and improves the quality of decision making made by humans.

Beyond the improved data collection, storage, retrieval and data analysis that computers can perform over humans, there is a desire to improve how a computer processes its input, with the intent to deliver more sophisticated output. To achieve this objective, computer science has been improving Artificial Intelligence in many areas such as autonomous vehicles, medical research, facilities management, data analytics, robotics, facial recognition, and even "natural-sounding synthetic speech from text like the Estonian language." (Fishel-Mihkla,n.d.)

Fundamentally computers are binary calculation devices that solve mathematical equations. A computer converts input it receives into binary data which is analyzed using mathematical algorithms. Artificial Intelligence is a general term that encompasses several ways to use computers to conduct specialized mathematical calculations that provide more sophisticated output. The objective of the various components of Artificial Intelligence is to improve the intrinsic value of the output it generates from input it receives. The data fed into a computer may be manually input by humans, input from other computing devices or retrieved by the system itself.

The Neuron

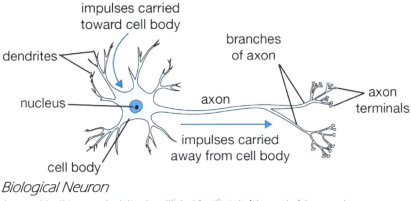

Biological Neuron
https://wiki.tum.de/display/lfdv/Artificial+Neural+Networks

"A nerve cell, or neuron, is a cell that receives information from other nerve cells or from the sensory organs and then projects that information to other nerve cells, while still other neurons project it back to the parts of the body that interact with the environment, such as the muscles". (National Research Council, p.116). More specifically, in a biological neuron, the dendrites of the neuron receive messages from other nerve cells or neurons, then transfer it to the nucleus of the neuron (also known as the soma) which processes the message then sends a response down the axon to other nerve cells' dendrites which in turn effects a reaction such as a muscle movement. The axon can also send it to the dendrites of another neuron for that cell's soma to process it further. The connection area between a sending axon and the receiving dendrite is known as the synapse. In biological entities, the synapse can be either an electrical or chemical connection between the two neurons. If a message is sent down the axon, to be forwarded out the neuron to another neuron, the synapse at the end of the axon, known as the axon terminals, will attempt to send either a chemical or electrical signal to another neuron's dendrite that also participates in the same synapse area.

Depending on the signal sent by the (presynaptic) neuron's axon terminal across the mutually shared synaptic region, the receiving neuron's (postsynaptic neuron) dendrite will either accept or reject the message.

In the world of Artificial Intelligence, the concept of a neuron exists, but how input is accepted is based on mathematical representation, not electrical or chemical stimuli as in a biological neuron.

After the Dartmouth AI conference Paul Rosenblatt-with inspiration from Warren McCulloch, Walter Pitts and Donald Hebb-formalized a conceptual perspective for an artificial neuron by defining a "perceptron" (CalState-LB, n.d.). The perceptron which Rosenblatt postulated in his book, Principles *of Neurodynamics*, was presented as the foundation for a visual recognition computer designed for the Department of Defense (DoD,1961).

Rosenblatt's perceptron theory provided a mathematical algorithm for a "brain model" (DoD, p.3) that accepts weighted input values that represents the priority of the input, adds a bias value with the resultant value(sum) determining the next action. For example, if the sum of the weighted inputs reaches a pre-defined threshold in the receiving neuron then the value will be accepted as an output for the perceptron, if not, the perceptron will ignore the inputs and not provide an output.

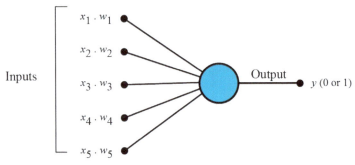

Artificial Neuron *(Perceptron)*

Beyond Rosenblatt's original perceptron design, additional mathematical operations are applied to a perceptron to enable it to function in a neural network. For example, a Sigmoid function, tanh and a Rectified Linear Unit (ReLU) calculation is applied to the values. These calculations are applied to the input weighted values to normalize the summed values to create what is known as the "Activation Function", which is the process to determine if a perceptron should send (activate) an output. (Osserman, 2017)

Rosenblatt's work on the DoD funded Perceptron Computer was not successful and the understanding of a perceptron was slow in coming. But over time his work for the DoD to create the core of a machine using a perceptron was revolutionary enough to be the seed for the creation of Artificial Intelligence.

To clarify, a perceptron is not a neuron in a traditional sense since it works by mathematical stimulation and not chemical or electrical stimulation like a biological neuron, however, it has become customary to refer to a perceptron as a neuron.

Artificial Neural Network

Like a Biological Neural Network (BNN) that is comprised of multiple interconnected neurons, an Artificial Neural Network (ANN) is an interconnected network of more than one artificial neuron (perceptron). In both a BNN and ANN, inputs or outputs to an individual neuron may be received from another neuron or from a non-neuron (stimulus), but a neuron must have at least one connection (input or output) to another neuron to be a part of a neural network.

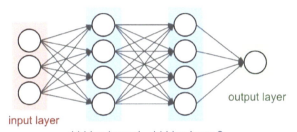

input layer

hidden layer 1   hidden layer 2

output layer

Image Courtesy of: http://cs231n.github.io/convolutional-networks/

In an ANN, if a neuron only accepts input from another neuron and outputs to another neuron, this is considered a "hidden layer". This distinction of a hidden layer is unique to ANN and does not apply to BNNs since "the human brain is not structured this way." (King, 2017), The impact of a hidden layer is important when it comes to understanding how an ANN must learn to improve the accuracy of its final output since there is a hidden layer that is not directly communicated with when providing feedback during training, thus techniques to modify the calculations done by the hidden neuron to improve its "intelligence" must be utilized.

Intelligence

The Oxford Dictionary defines "intelligence" as "The ability to acquire and apply knowledge and skills". To acquire knowledge and skills, an entity must learn. Therefore, learning is key to intelligence.

To derive an output, an artificial neuron accepts weighted mathematical values inputs from other neurons or external systems. The neuron processes these values using a form of linear algebra (Specifically Matrices) and the resultant sum is passed to another neuron or an external system, such as sensory neurons. If the output of a neuron is incorrect, a method must exist to modify the incorrect value.

To help derive the proper output, a neuron or ANN can be programed the response algorithm in advance (hard coded), which is fine for simple decision tasks. However, for more complex decisions, programming the path to determine a correct output may be too difficult. In fact, being able to eliminate the requirement to predefine an outcome is one of the key capabilities of Artificial Intelligence. If properly trained, an ANN can process larger amounts of information, more complex variables, all at a faster rate than a static computer program or a BNN.

When the output of a neuron is not programmed in advance, other models for learning can be utilized. The general models for learning are known as supervised learning, unsupervised learning, semi-supervised learning and Reinforcement Learning (RL). These models can be used for a neuron to learn the correct output (Rodriquez,2017)

Supervised learning is a method of learning "that uses a known dataset (called the training dataset) to make predictions". (MathWorks-Supervised Learning, n.d.) One supervised learning technique used to train an ANN is known as a Feed Forward Network (FFN). An FFN uses a known dataset, referred to as "Labeled Data", which is a paired set of data that contains an input value with its correct output value. The input data is fed into a Neural Network (NN) and the final output from the NN is compared to the correct value. If the output is incorrect, the weights(bias) of the input values will be adjusted. The complete process from initial input into a NN to the final output of the NN is referred to an "epoch of learning". (djmw,2004) The epoch will be repeated until the final output value is correct.

Another learning technique, known as Backward Propagation can also be used for supervised learning of a NN and a Deep Learning (DL) network. A DL network is essentially an ANN that is trained using very large datasets (MathWorks-Deep Learning, n.d.). Backward propagation is a process that attempts to send back (back propagate) recommend adjustment values to the neurons in the neural network (Robin,2009). The method works by repeating the epoch, comparing the actual output to the expected value, then using gradient descent and linear regression to modify the value to descend (close the gap) the actual output value towards the expected output value. (Nedrich, 2014)

There are two main approaches a supervised learning model uses for its datasets. The first type of use for a dataset is for use in a regression analysis model, such as a backward propagation or a deep learning network which are used for iterative learning. The second approach for using a dataset is called classification. In classification, there are groupings of similar data defined upfront and subsequent data is predicated relative to a predefined group. When a variation occurs from the expected result (i.e. predication inaccuracy) a value or weight is determined then applied to adjust the prediction in subsequent inputs. This approach is favored for the FFN technique.

Another supervised learning methodology is the Support Vector Machines (SVM). An SVM supervised learning method uses both clustering of multiple dimensional data points and regression analysis of the multi-dimensional dataset. The benefit of this two-group approach is greater accuracy and reduced training times. Instead of basing training only on single groupings (clustering) of similar data or iterative training to reduce variance (regression analysis), SVM looks to "formulate the problem in a difference space" (Phillips, p.804) by seeking optimal adherence to both clustering and regression analysis simultaneously.

Unsupervised learning-unlike supervised learning-does not use a predefined input or output dataset to compare values going in or coming out of the neurons. With unsupervised learning, data is fed (input) into the neuron or ANN and "Unsupervised learning algorithms group the data in an unlabeled data set based on the underlying hidden features in the data", (Jones,2017) It is this method of self-identifying patterns that has led to the discovery of previously unknown patterns in data when using AI to conduct the analysis of large datasets.

In security, unsupervised learning is the conceptual foundation for the creation of Generative Adversarial

Networks (GAN). GANs have been used to create malicious software (Malware) for nefarious purposes and as a tool to protect against malicious software. These unsupervised learning networks are referred to as MalGANs. (Weiwei-Ying,2017)

Semi-supervised learning, as its name implies, is a hybrid or combination of learning methods where known datasets (labeled data) are used with unknown datasets (unlabeled data). "The goal of semi-supervised learning is to understand how combining labeled and unlabeled data may change the learning behavior, and to design algorithms that take advantage of such a combination."(Xiaojin-Goldberg,2009) This method of learning is more akin to how BNNs work, meaning humans are typically presented with information, they understand part of it from prior learning, but there may be a part of the information that requires them to learn how to respond to it. An example of information presented that is a combination of old and new knowledge happens when learning a new skill or traveling to an unfamiliar area.

Reinforcement Learning is "a goal-oriented learning based on interaction with [an] environment". (Shaikh,2017). The distinguishing characteristic RL has over supervised, unsupervised and semi-supervised learning is that a feedback or "reward function" (Shaikh,2017) exists that can be used to independently improve the values (weights) of the inputs.

As previously mentioned, computers can identify patterns and interrelationships in data previously unknown, especially when analyzing large datasets. Along with their ability to solve problems that require analysis of large datasets, the analysis they perform, with any size dataset, is done much faster than humanly capable. If an AI system can evaluate its inputs and outputs independently it can self-achieve accuracy. Interestingly, along with its self-improvement, it can offer output improvements to the system it is sending its data. For example, Google's AutoML AI attempts to first learn the required proper outputs for a given AI target, once it is successful, it will then seek to modify its AI target or create a "child" object with the experience it has gained during its RL phase (Galeon-Houser, 2017). An example of creating and improving an AI child is Google's AutoML improvement to its NASNet. NASNet is a Machine Learning (ML) based AI child to Google's AutoML. (Google Brain Team, 2017).

An example of an ML based AI modifying its output, to improve its quality was the result of an experiment conducted by Facebook researchers in the Facebook AI Research Lab (FAIR) with two chatbots(*https://aws.amazon.com/what-is-a-chatbot/*). The researcher's setup up two chatbots to talk to each other unrestricted. After a brief span of time of independent communications, the chatbots modified their outputs to improve how they communicated with each other. Interestingly, the communication protocol they developed may have been optimal for them and allowed them to communicate more efficiently, it was incomprehensible to humans. (Griffin, 2017)

Appendix A

Bibliography

1. Carey, M. (2018). *Artificial Intelligence Facial Recognition Threat Detection Environment (Artificial Intelligence Architectures.* Lexington, KY. Amazon Publishing.
2. Moral Robots (n.d.). Making sense of robot ethics. Retrieved from: https://moral-robots.com/philosophy/aristotles-ai/
3. History-Computer (n.d.). Thomas Hobbes. Retrieved from: http://history-computer.com/Dreamers/Hobbes.html
4. Foote, K.D. (2016, April 5). A Brief History of Artificial Intelligence. Dataversity. Retrieved from: http://www.dataversity.net/brief-history-artificial-intelligence/
5. Kapp, S. (2006, July 24). Artificial Intelligence: Past, Present, and Future. VOX of Dartmouth. Retrieved from: http://www.dartmouth.edu/~vox/0607/0724/ai50.html
6. World-Information (n.d.).1960s-1970s: Increased Research in Artificial Intelligence (AI). Retrieved from: http://world-information.org/wio/infostructure/100437611663/100438659474
7. Wheeler, A. (2017, August 25). NVIDIA's Artificial Intelligence Boom: What Makes AI and GPU so Compatible? Engineering.com. Retrieved from: https://www.engineering.com/Hardware/ArticleI

D/15471/NVIDIAs-Artificial-Intelligence-Boom-
What-Makes-AI-and-GPUs-so-Compatible.aspx

8. Fishel,M.,Mihkla,M.(n.d.). Modelling the temporal
    structure of newsreaders' speech on neural
    networks for Estonian text-to-speech synthesis.
    Institute of Estonian Language, University of Tartu.
    Retrieved from:
    https://pdfs.semanticscholar.org/8cb9/d38ab791fe560
    8da8e9b0a00393185ab24c3.pdf

9. National Research Council (2000). How People
    Learn: Brain, Mind, Experience, and School:
    Expanded Edition. Washington DC: The National
    Academies Press. https://doi.org/10.17226/9853

10. CalState-LB (n.d.). History of the Perceptron.
    California State University, Long Beach. Retrieved
    from:
    https://web.csulb.edu/~cwallis/artificialn/History.h
    tm

11. DoD (1961, March 15). PRINCIPLES OF
    NEURODYNAMICS. PERCEPTRONS AND THE
    THEORY OF BRAIN MECHANISMS. Frank
    Rosenblatt, Director, Cognitive Systems Research
    Program, Cornell University for the Department of
    Defense, Contract Monr-2381(00). UNCLASSIFIED.
    Retrieved from:
    http://www.dtic.mil/dtic/tr/fulltext/u2/256582.pdf

12. Osserman,H.(2017, June 27). Aspects of Deep
    Learning: Activation Functions. x.ai. Retrieved
    from: https://x.ai/blog/aspects-of-deep-learning-
    activation-functions/

13. King, P. (2017, May 21). How many hidden layers
    are in the neural network of the human brain?
    Quora. Retrieved from:
    https://www.quora.com/How-many-hidden-

layers-are-in-the-neural-network-of-the-human-brain

14. Rodriquez, J. (2017, January 19). *Types of Artificial Intelligence Learning Models.* Medium. Retrieved from: https://medium.com/@jrodthoughts/types-of-artificial-intelligence-learning-models-814e46eca30e

15. MathWorks-Supervised Learning. (n.d.). *Supervised Learning.* Retrieved from: https://www.mathworks.com/discovery/supervised-learning.html

16. djmw (2004, April 28). *Feedforward neural networks 1.1. The learning phase.* University of Amsterdam. Retrieved from: http://www.fon.hum.uva.nl/praat/manual/Feedforward_neural_networks_1_1__The_learning_phase.html

17. MathWorks-Deep Learning (n.d.). *What is Deep Learning? 3 things you need to know.* Retrieved from: https://www.mathworks.com/discovery/deep-learning.html

18. Robin (2009, November 26). BACKPROPOGATION. *Artificial Intelligence. Articles on Artificial Intelligence.* Retrieved from: http://intelligence.worldofcomputing.net/machine-learning/learning-by-back-propagation.html#.WtoUuYjwZhE

19. Nedrich, M. (2014, June 24). *An Introduction to Gradient Descent and Linear Regression.* Atomic Object. Retrieved from: https://spin.atomicobject.com/2014/06/24/gradient-descent-linear-regression/

20. Phillips, P.J. (n.d.). Support Vector Machines Applied to Face Recognition. *National Institute of Standards and Technology.* Retrieved from: https://papers.nips.cc/paper/1609-support-vector-machines-applied-to-face-recognition.pdf

21. Jones, M.T. (2017, December 4). Unsupervised learning for data classification. *IBM.* Retrieved from: https://www.ibm.com/developerworks/library/cc-unsupervised-learning-data-classification/index.html

22. Weiwei,H. Ying,T. (2017, February 20). Generating Adversarial Malware Examples for Black-Box Attacks Based on GAN. *Department of Machine Intelligence, Peking University.* Retrieved from: http://www.cil.pku.edu.cn/publications/papers/2017/MalGAN_IJCAI_2017_Hu_Tan.pdf

23. Xiaojin,Z., Goldberg,A.B.(2009). Introduction to Semi-Supervised Learning. *Synthesis Lectures on Artificial Intelligence and Machine Learning.* Retrieved from: https://www.morganclaypool.com/doi/abs/10.2200/S00196ED1V01Y200906AIM006?journalCode=aim

24. Shaikh,F.(2017, January 19). Simple Beginner's guide to Reinforcement Learning & its implementation. *Analytics Vidhya.* Retrieved from: https://www.analyticsvidhya.com/blog/2017/01/introduction-to-reinforcement-learning-implementation/

25. Galeon, D., Houser, K. (2017, December 1). Google's Artificial Intelligence Built and AI That Outperforms Any Made by Humans. *Futurism.* https://futurism.com/google-artificial-intelligence-built-ai/

26. Google Brain Team (2017, November 2). AutoML for large scale image classification and object detection. Retrieved from: https://research.googleblog.com/2017/11/autom l-for-large-scale-image.html
27. Griffin, A. (2017, July 31). Facebook's Artificial Intelligence Robots Shut Down After They Start Talking to Each Other In Their Own Language. Independent. Retrieved from: https://www.independent.co.uk/life-style/gadgets-and-tech/news/facebook-artificial-intelligence-ai-chatbot-new-language-research-openai-google-a7869706.html

Appendix B

Russia Conference on "Artificial Intelligence: Problems and ways to solve them-2018"

The following information document was retrieved from the Ministry of Defense of the Russian Federation and translated into English:

Retrieved from: *http://mil.ru/conferences/is-intellekt.htm*

Conference "Artificial Intelligence: Problems and Solutions" - 2018 "

On March 14-15, 2018, the Ministry of Defense of the Russian Federation together with the Ministry of Education and Science of the Russian Federation and the Russian Academy of Sciences organized and held a conference on "Artificial Intelligence: Problems and ways to solve them - 2018 ".

The plenary and sectional wills of the conference presented reports on a wide range of issues that reveal the current state and the main directions of development of artificial intelligence in the Russian Federation and abroad.

Conference participants noted that fundamental and exploratory research in the field of artificial intelligence in our country is carried out at a high scientific level, not inferior to the world.

Considering that the leading role of states in the modern information society is largely determined by the level of development of information technologies, first of all, the technologies of intellectual analysis and decision support at various levels of government, including the military sphere, as well as significant scientific and technological groundwork in Russia in the field of artificial intelligence systems the conference recommends:

1. The Russian Academy of Sciences together with the Ministry of Education and Science of Russia, the FAU of Russia, the Ministry of Industry and Trade of Russia and the Ministry of Defense of Russia to consider the proposals of Moscow State University. MVLomonosova and FITS IU RAS to create a consortium on the problems of analyzing big data and artificial intelligence in order to combine the efforts of leading scientific, educational and industrial organizations to create and implement artificial intelligence technologies.

2. The Russian Academy of Sciences together with the Ministry of Education and Science of the Russian Federation, the Ministry of Industry and Trade of Russia and the Ministry of Defense of Russia to step up work on creating and filling the Foundation of analytical algorithms and programs to ensure high-quality expertise of the proposed solutions in the interests of automated systems for various purposes.

3. The Ministry of Education and Science of Russia together with the Russian Academy of Sciences and the Ministry of Defense of Russia to prepare proposals on the creation of a state system for training and retraining specialists in the field of artificial intelligence, including, in particular, obtaining a second education for specialists in other areas of the economy.

4. The Ministry of Defense of Russia together with the FANO of Russia, Moscow State University. MVLomonoyeva and FITS IU RAS to study the issue of creating a laboratory in VIT "ERA" for testing promising software and hardware

solutions in the field of creating artificial intelligence by the operators of scientific companies.

5. The Russian Academy of Sciences, in conjunction with the Advanced Research Foundation, will prepare proposals for the creation of a National Center for Artificial Intelligence, which will contribute to the creation of a scientific reserve, the development of an innovative infrastructure in the field of artificial intelligence, and the implementation of theoretical research results and promising projects in artificial intelligence and GG technologies.

6. The Ministry of Defense of Russia, together with the Ministry of Education and Science of the Russian Federation and the Russian Academy of Sciences, in the interests of organizing a full account of the long-term and medium-term trends in the development of artificial intelligence, as well as monitoring changes occurring in the field of artificial intelligence in other countries, organize research on the entire range of issues related to development of artificial intelligence, including social science.

7. The Russian Ministry of Defense to organize the preparation and conduct of a series of military games, on a wide range of scenarios, with the definition of the influence of artificial intelligence models on the changing nature of the conduct of hostilities in various options at the tactical, operational and strategic levels.

8. The Foundation for Advanced Studies, in conjunction with the Russian Academy of Sciences, the Ministry of Education and Science of the Russian Federation and the Federal Agency of Scientific Organizations of Russia, should prepare proposals for creating a system for

assessing the compliance of intellectual technologies with the requirements in the Russian Federation.

9. The above proposals should be considered in the scientific business program of the International Military-Technical Forum Army-2018 and the International Forum "National Security Week" with the participation of all interested federal executive bodies (August 21-26, 2018).

10. To recommend the Russian Academy of Sciences, the Ministry of Education and Science of the Russian Federation and the Ministry of Defense of Russia to provide for the annual holding of the Conference on Artificial Intelligence.

Appendix C

Generative Adversarial Network and MalGAN

Machine Learning systems can be fooled (Gershgorn,2016). Since the begging of computing, there are those who try and figure out how to effect unintended behavior in computing systems or programs. This risk becomes greater when using a system that learns from human and other program behavior since the learning system cannot normally discern between legitimate and illegitimate behavior. A technique growing in popularity to assist in evaluating the reliability and accuracy of AI systems is automated testing using other AI based systems to generate incorrect data and examine the target AI system's response to the data known as adversarial data. The AI system generating the adversarial data (known as the Generator) and the targeted system (known as the Black Box) are placed on the same data network so they can communicate. This environment is known as a Generative Adversarial Network or GAN. The AI system generating the adversarial data will modify the data being sent to the black box with variations that include good data, nonsensical data (noise) and the malware itself. The response of the black-box to the data will be examined for its identification accuracy. The use of a GAN helps with testing the target by generating more sample perturbations and sending them at a far faster rate than a human is capable. Ideally a Deep Learning based adversarial generator is used so it can draw upon enormous amounts of data to create its samples. In both an unsupervised and reinforced learning scenario what the black box learns can be feed back into the black box's ANN.

A paper at the 2018 International Conference on Learning Representations (ICL) proposes refinement to the generation of adversarial samples to help refine how the black-box classifies what it receives (Anonymous, n.d.). The authors point out that much of the adversarial data generation for black-box testing has used extreme variations, which does not accurately represent what these systems are more likely to see in production. They propose generating adversarial examples that contain minor or common errors they call "Natural Adversarial Examples" (Anonymous, n.d.). This method is more applicable to techniques used in polymorphic or metamorphic malware (Hosmer,2008) types where changes to malware code and their decryptors can be subtle, yet enough to evade recognition using signature identification, heuristics or normal pattern recognition.

Below are two examples of GANs established to generate and evaluate samples of Malware and as such are referred to as MalGANs.

Two Dimensional Malware Generative Adversarial Network

With a two-dimensional GAN there is the adversarial generator and the black-box on the network. The black box is examined for its detection accuracy.

A variation on this is a three-dimensional GAN where a "Detector" is used on the far side of the black-box. In this model the black-box is acting in a gateway malware inspection device for the detector. The black-box is architected to forward the received malware sample from the generator to the detector if the sample is interpreted as safe by the black box, otherwise it blocks the malware sample. This GAN speeds up evaluation since only the detector must be examined. Also, the detector can be used for unsupervised and reinforced learning for the black box and its data feedback to the black box for reinforced training. It is also a more accurate representation of how data security systems are implemented as gateways and not store and forward as in the two-dimensional MalGAN design.

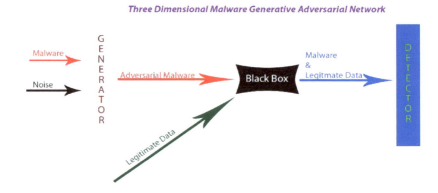

Three Dimensional Malware Generative Adversarial Network

Weiwei Hu and Ying Tan of the Peking University conducted a formal study to test the effectiveness of using an AI MalGAN to bypass an AI based malware detector (Weiwei & Ying, 2017). They approached the challenge in a different manner that was done by other researchers examining AI and malware penetration. Previous researchers have used AI to focus solely on improving defensive software's accuracy rate of malware detection. Instead Weiwei and Ying focused on using a MalGAN to improve the robustness of AI malware generators to avoid black box detection. They found even if using sets of information to train the black box detectors, their MalGAN system was able to pass nearly all their samples through the black box to the detector within a short timeframe. Even if they trained the black box with their malware samples, their MalGAN could still penetrate the black box and reach the detector in again, a brief period. In repeated tests they were able to get their AI generated malware samples to the detector in the high 90th percentile.

Appendix C

Bibliography

1. Gershgorn,D. (2016, March 30). Fooling The Machine. Byzantine science of deceiving artificial intelligence. Popular Science. Retrieved from: https://www.popsci.com/byzantine-science-deceiving-artificial-intelligence
2. Anonymous, (n.d.). Generating Natural Adversarial Examples. Under review as a conference paper at ICLR 2018. Retrieved from: https://openreview.net/pdf?id=H1BLjgZCb
3. Hosmer,C. (2008). Polymorphic & Metamorphic Malware. Wetstone. Retrieved from: https://www.blackhat.com/presentations/bh-usa-08/Hosmer/BH_US_08_Hosmer_Polymorphic_Malware.pdf
4. Weiwei,H. Ying,T. (2017, February 20). Generating Adversarial Malware Examples for Black-Box Attacks Based on GAN. Department of Machine Intelligence, Peking University. Retrieved from: http://www.cil.pku.edu.cn/publications/papers/2017/MalGAN_IJCAI_2017_Hu_Tan.pdf

Appendix D

Analytics Maturity Model

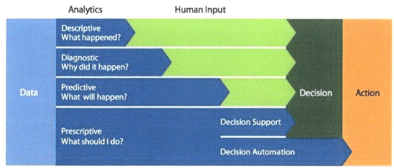

Source: Gartner, #G00254653 (September 2013)

Image Courtesy:

https://www.ibm.com/developerworks/community/blogs/jfp/resource/BLOGS_UPLOADED_IMAGES/analytics_maturity1.png